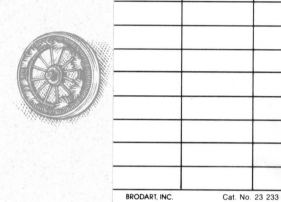

S

M28

MAY 5 1993

4965

Contents

Introduction

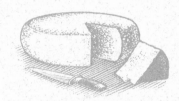

This anthology of told stories is the product of a remarkable oral history project conceived to commemorate International Literacy Year, 1990.

In the spring of 1990, twenty-eight adult literacy groups from all parts of Ontario undertook to collect the stories of people in their communities using the techniques of oral history. The aim of the undertaking was two-fold: to promote literacy among the participants and at the same time to retrieve and preserve the histories of people and communities that are seldom given much acknowledgement in the mainstream historical record. The stories in this book are the authentic voices of Native people in Thunder Bay and Golden Lake, women in Kingston and Killaloe, deaf people in Toronto, people with disabilities in Smith's Falls, immigrants in Dryden and Toronto, Mexican Mennonites in Chatham, and farming people in Palmer Rapids.

Through the hearing, taping, and transcribing of other people's spoken words, the adult learners who

were the primary researchers in the project were able to make significant strides in their mastery of reading and writing and in their exploration and understanding of their own histories and the history of their communities.

This experiment was based first of all on the conviction that learning to read and write, like all learning, can be meaningful and effective only if it is linked directly to the real life of the learner. Secondly, it was believed that the power of the spoken word could attract people of all backgrounds and language skills through a fundamental and natural human love—the telling and hearing of stories.

In the view of oral historians, history is not just, or even primarily, what is said and done by the prominent and the powerful; it is also the story of our collective past—life as it was lived and perceived by the vast majority of men and women. It is this rich store of experience that is mined by oral historians in their attempt to create a historical record that not only encompasses, but also celebrates the everyday life of the ordinary man and woman in all its richness and variety. Oral history places the experience of the common man and woman at the centre of the historical stage. And this view of and approach to history has important implications not only for our understanding of history but also for our philosophy of education.

In its valuing of the "common experience", oral history makes history accessible to ordinary people. Stories of experiences lived, of events witnessed, of observations made become the stuff of history. One need not be an academic historian or even literate to listen to or understand the shared stories and accounts of personal testimony. Such stories, however, can be the basis for a form of learning that is at once personal and empowering. The link, then, between oral history and literacy is both more simple and more complex than it would at first appear, rooted as it is in the value that oral history places on the personal testimonies of ordinary people and in the way it views their relationship to history.

In recent years, literacy has come to be viewed in Canada and around the world as more than simply the capacity to read and write. It is now seen by many as an essential catalyst for personal growth and political empowerment. This view has in fact become a fundamental precept in popular education. The key to this approach is the linking of learning to personal experience in a way that allows the learner to explore critically the social, cultural, economic, and political realities with which he or she must live. Learning and literacy can thus become agents for social change.

In popular education, "language experience" is a strategy used in literacy work to link learning to the real issues and concerns in the learners' daily lives. In this approach, learners are encouraged to tell stories that are based on or related to their own experience. The stories are then transcribed and used as the text for developing reading and writing skills. In this way, the experience of the learner is placed at the centre of the learning process. The International Literacy Year Oral History Project was a blending of this method in popular education with the practices of oral history.

Throughout this project, it was the adult learners who occupied centre stage. It was they who chose the subjects for their oral history projects, who conducted interviews with the storytellers, who gathered relevant documentation, and who taped and transcribed the stories. It was also they who chose the stories to be submitted for consideration by the editors of this anthology, as many more stories were gathered than could be included in one volume. The original tapes of the stories collected from over twenty-five communities across the province are to be included in the collections of the Archives of Ontario.

The spirit and goals of the International Literacy Year Oral History Project were supported by grants and resources from the Literacy Branch of the Ministry of Education, the Archives of Ontario, and the National Literacy Secretariat. In addition, countless individuals and organizations in the participating communities gave valuable assistance. Information about the projects and the participants can be found at the back of the book.

The stories included in this anthology are but a few of the many testimonies and tales contributed by men and women from all walks of life and from all regions of Ontario. As such, they speak all the more eloquently for the immense wealth of experience and cultural diversity that underly the history of this province. Those who gave their time and talent to this project have salvaged something of this wealth for future generations and made us all richer as a result.

Literacy Branch
Ministry of Education, Ontario

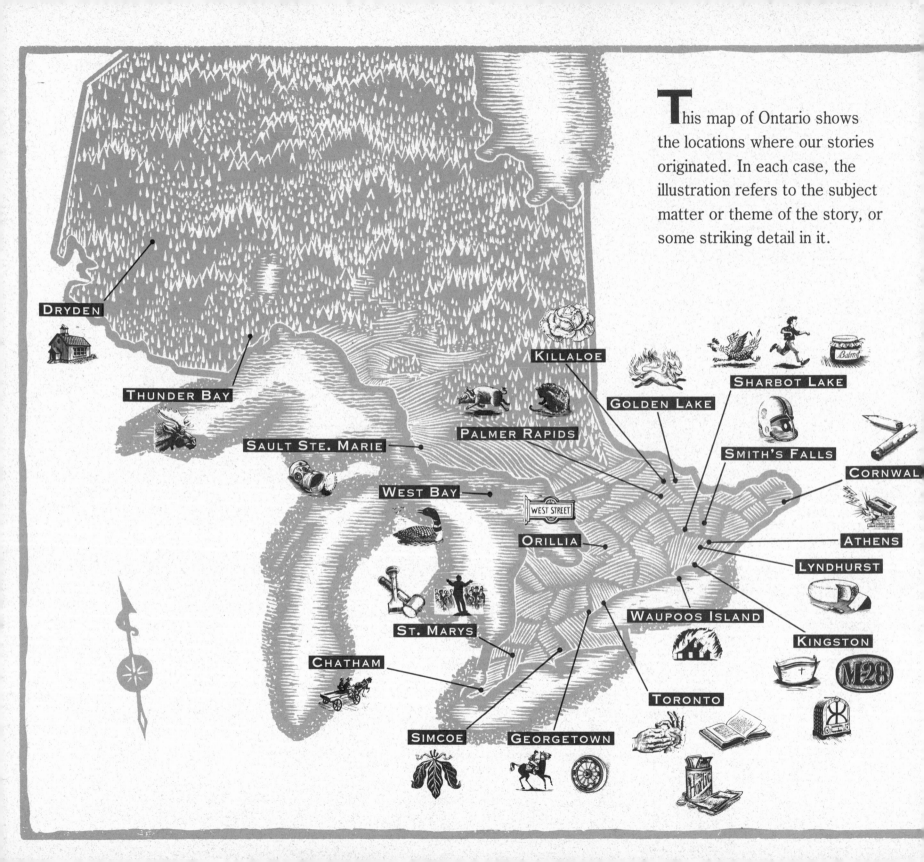

This map of Ontario shows the locations where our stories originated. In each case, the illustration refers to the subject matter or theme of the story, or some striking detail in it.

DRYDEN

THUNDER BAY

SAULT STE. MARIE

WEST BAY

WEST STREET

KILLALOE

PALMER RAPIDS

GOLDEN LAKE

SHARBOT LAKE

SMITH'S FALLS

CORNWAL

ATHENS

LYNDHURST

ORILLIA

ST. MARYS

CHATHAM

WAUPOOS ISLAND

KINGSTON

TORONTO

SIMCOE

GEORGETOWN

The Stories

We brought together twenty-nine stories to make this book.

To find the stories, we brought together hundreds of people from every region of Ontario. One of our aims was to capture the diversity of experiences that has always characterized our vast province.

Some people told stories that they had told many times before; others told new stories that surprised even themselves. What is not surprising is that most of the stories are about people or about people's communities. Yet each person told a story no one else could tell.

Listen to the stories. More than that, listen to the voices. Yes, *listen*—because these are "told" stories. They will make more sense if you read them out loud. And they will be truer.

As you listen, ask yourself the question: Does the person make the story or does the story make the person? You be the judge.

The Head of the Clan

Long before most of the people who now inhabit our province came to Ontario, the Anishnabe, one of the First Nations people, told each other stories. Passed on from generation to generation, many of these stories, like this one from West Bay, are alive today.

A long time ago, the Loon and the Crane were both strong leaders within their clan, but the Loon wanted to be the head of the clan. The Loon challenged the Crane. The Crane did not want to fight for this position. The Crane and the other birds realized it was a lot of work to be a leader and to accept so much responsibility.

The Loon was very proud to be looked upon as the leader. Everyone looked to him for advice and guidance.

It was not long before the birds were not happy with the Loon and his ways of dealing with the problems. The birds wanted to leave for the south, but the Loon was not ready. The birds had to wait. By the time the Loon was ready to go, many of the birds had suffered hardships. Many had died by remaining too long.

When the Loon finally began the migration south, there were still many complaints about the speed, the height, and the distances travelled daily. Upon arrival in the south, there were others who wanted to go further south. The Loon tried to consider the well-being of all and refused.

Without saying any more, they left the Loon.

The birds wanted the Loon to resign his position. The malcontents argued, "You have little concern for our differences or our needs. You are indifferent to our hardships." The Loon countered, "The well-being of all comes first. I have to consider the general good." The Bluebird retorted, "The general good has almost killed us all." Still the Loon replied, "I must think of all, not just one or just a few." The other birds groaned, "You think too big. In thinking too big, you forgot the small." Without saying any more, they left the Loon.

Alone, the Loon thought about his period of leadership. The role of a leader seemed a lot of work and involved making decisions for many people. A leader is expected to seek and rely on the opinions of the whole group. The Loon resigned his position. And the Crane was made the head of the clan. ∽

There Was a Witch

This story took place in Golden Lake about a hundred years ago, but it could be anywhere and anytime. . . . It's a story of jealousy and mother love, courage and witchcraft.

When my father went to hunt we would all get into bed with my mother, all three of us—Katie and Jenny and I—and Mother would tell us stories.

Now they don't believe such a thing happened, but there was a witch—my mother told me about that. This witch witched my mother because she married my father when this other woman wanted to marry him. So this other woman was mad at my mother and she got her witched. This witch came from Combermere, somewhere in the bush; she lived there somewhere in a log cabin.

Anyway, my mother got sick shortly after they were married. She got real sick; she couldn't get out of bed, she couldn't eat, she brought up everything she ate. And they used to see a fox, a fox coming down the lakeshore, there where we lived down by the dam. This fox would walk down the shore all on fire. It was all on fire. They would shoot at it and never hit it. The fox would just

run into the bush. My grandmother would say, "That is the witch! She is doing that—that is the witch's work! I am going after her!"

So she got a little bundle together, a lunch. And she had a little tomahawk—she always carried that tomahawk—and she took it and went after the witch that lived in Combermere. She walked all the way there, and she got to where the witch lived.

Luckily . . . the witch was sleeping.

Luckily the door was locked and the witch was sleeping. It was at night. Grandmother went in and woke the witch up and told her about my mother being sick. She said, "I know who is doing that, and that is you! And if you don't cure her," she said, "you see this axe? One blow of this and there will be no more of you!"

The old lady got up out of bed. "Come on, you, come with me," she said to my grandmother. "We'll go and get the medicine." So she got a light, what they called a "slut". They went in the bush, in the dark, for a long time, and she finally got the root. And the old woman said, "You go home and wash this good, and boil this, and give this to your daughter. She will get better."

My grandmother had something to eat and she walked right back, all the way back here. She came home and made that medicine and she gave it to my mother, and in a couple days my mother got better. And the old fox was still going walking along, and they still didn't hit it; they could never hit it. But in a couple more days the fox quit coming, so my mother got better.

And that witch came back here and she had a tent somewhere. And they said whenever she wanted to witch someone, you would see that old tent shaking, that old tent shaking. That was when she was witching somebody. So they got rid of her; they got her to leave and not come back.

So that is the witch story that was really true.

Respect for the Moose

After the hunt, when the fire is burning and the feast is about to begin, the hunter tells the story of the hunt. So bite into a good moose-nose sandwich and listen to this hunting story from Thunder Bay.

Last year I went out moose hunting. We went out because we didn't have enough money for turkey, so we decided to get moose meat instead.

We came from here—Thunder Bay. The time was around eleven o'clock at night. We went up Spruce River Road, on the road to Armstrong, and on the way back, that's when I shot one, about an hour and half up the road, way past Madaline Mines. Coming back, that's when I shot one, for turkey dinner. Coming back this way, just looking out of the window, I said, "Woah, woah, stop! There's a moose there!" It was standing there in the gully, standing in the moonlight. I'm not using a spotlight, nothing. Not even gloves. I got off there, with my gun—a 303—with five shots in the clip. I took my time loading up, real slow. The moose was pretty close to one hundred yards away. I wasn't excited.

Some guys get really excited, but not me; I've been hunting all my life.

You got to concentrate on your shooting, then you don't get nervous. Just say, "Holy shit! I'd better not miss!" Think in your head. As soon as you know you got him dead on, you squeeze the trigger.

We boil the nose . . . until it's soft.

When you see a moose standing, then you gotta be level with the moose, bend your knees a little bit, dead even with the moose. If you're standing straight up, then you'll be either above or below the moose with your shot. You have to bend your knees a little bit. I see a lot of guys miss like that, standing up straight.

When the moose drops you feel good, you feel happy, you think you don't have to waste more bullets. You think about eating moose meat; we had a nice feast that day.

After the moose drops we have a smoke break, sharpen our knives. Even in the middle of winter, right before New Year's Day. It was cold, my hair was grey with frost and I'm sweating at the same time. Even though it's cold, I'm excited, I guess, from shooting the moose. Some guys get cold easy. I ask them, "Why do you want to hunt when you get cold like that? You're not supposed to get cold, you're an Indian. What kind of Indian are you anyway?" That time I was wearing a thin jacket only, no gloves, nothing, but I wasn't cold.

I cut the arse end off, then pull out all the guts. You cut around the arse really good, then you just pull out all the guts, and then you cut open the rest of the moose. Then you cut into hindquarters, at the hips, at the shoulders, both sides, in a circle. We take almost everything—the nose and the tongue, too.

We boil the nose, boil it until it's soft, about two to three hours. If you cook it for only an hour, it tastes and feels like rubber; you gotta cook it around three hours, then we make a sandwich with it. When it's cold outside, a moose-nose sandwich tastes really good.

The tongue we fry with onions—that tastes good, too. The meat doesn't last very long because you give the meat away—to family, to friends. Some meat, you make smoked meat out of it.

Before we leave the place where we cut up the moose, we take the hide and put the guts inside it and then we bury it. This was the way my dad did it; next time he went out hunting, then he gets a moose out of it. If you don't do this, then you won't get anything when you go out hunting. This is to show respect for the moose.

What Started the Fuss

Not every hunting story has a happy ending. A town like Sharbot Lake can be more dangerous than the bush if you're lost and hungry.

Well, my mother died when I was only one year old, and my father had to take us all around to different relations to keep us while he worked. We were at Aunt Mary-Ann's, or Uncle Tom and Uncle George's, and everybody else. We done all our visiting while we were young.

My father didn't know what to do; he couldn't stay at home all the time and watch us. We were alone a lot—that's why they brought us to the home. People getting inquisitive, wondering why the children were always running around and nobody at home.

There were no industries, he had to work wherever he could get it. Maybe it was working for the railroad. Maybe he'd be gone all winter, eh? Maybe he'd be gone all summer. We'd be left with somebody, and they'd leave us at their house and go about their work, and that's why we got lost, eh? We were at home lots of times for days and there was nobody there. We didn't have anything to eat, either.

I think what struck them was when we got the neighbour's chicken and cut his head off and cooked it up for dinner. It tasted good, what part we didn't burn of it. My older brother cut the chicken's head off—I'd probably have cut it in two. Cooking it was quite a job; I didn't know nothing about it. Don't know if we cooked it, roasted it, or burnt it.

After that they come and took us away.

I think that's what started the fuss, anyway. After that they come and took us away. I think our neighbour put in a complaint. He was afraid if we took that chicken, we'd be after another one. We were running around hungry half the time. We were at the store trying to get something. We were going here and there and all over. Well, you know children—they'll go anyplace, ask for anything.

If they'd have left us alone, we'd probably killed another one. Maybe cooked it better. I think that's why they sent us to the home. They reported it, and the Children's Aid come and took us to the home. They took several other children from Sharbot Lake, too. They sort of cleaned up the works. ∽

Slowly Surfacing

Some families have been in Ontario for generations, but new families arrive each year and add their stories to our story. Some are stories of hardship because change is never easy. This woman from Dryden found it difficult to have to see her children suffer.

We immigrated in '63 and we paid our own way. We didn't owe anybody any money, but we started off from scratch here again. It was August 30 in 1963 when we arrived in Dryden.

The beginning of September my children were enrolled in school. I started to really worry, because all of a sudden my children didn't talk, they didn't say anything. I thought, "My goodness! Have they gone mute?" But the reason was—because they couldn't speak English they felt sort of . . . resentful. My son was put two grades back, and he came home and blurted out, "Why am I put back? I wasn't dumb in school. I was doing well. Why is it happening to me?"

That's when I started to worry, because we easily could have lost them, they could have gotten into trouble. They maybe could have resented the school badly enough—they could have never even accomplished anything.

My daughter was very determined to go back. The grandparents were writing letters like, "If that's not working out, just come back, we'll help you," and that didn't help me in trying to make a go. The children were very close to their grandparents. My husband is the only son, and their grandmother was sending the children off to school in Germany every day when I was working. After they got off school I was back home, but still she was in close contact with them every day, and therefore the closeness was there. They missed her very much. We were all homesick.

If I would have had the money, I would have went back.

I have to admit, in the first six years if I would have had the money, I would have went back. It was because I saw the kids suffer, and that hurt me so much. I didn't want them to go through that.

But then I noticed things were picking up. My kids were becoming fluent and they were starting to like school. They were getting friends—good friends—and bringing their friends home. I was getting feeling better about the whole thing. My husband had a good job, and then money was coming in.

A pound of butter was seventy-five cents, a loaf of bread was fifteen cents, a package of cigarettes—my husband smoked then—was only fifty-six cents. My children were able to buy a chocolate bar with five cents. Then things started to pick up and prices started to rise, but of course the wages did too. When I started to work at the restaurant, at first I only got eighty-five cents an hour, then it went up to a dollar. I thought, "Gee, now I'm really getting somewhere." We were slowly surfacing.

My Father Was a Go-Getter

Many immigrants came to Ontario as adults; others came as children with their parents. This man came to Toronto as a little boy with his ambitious father, who was determined to make good.

I came to Canada when I was five years of age, arrived on May 24. My dad sold all the furniture—just brought the bare essentials like his books and a few clothing, and things he'd want to hang onto. But we sold the organ, sold the furniture, sold my toys. . . . Sold just about everything.

My father was a go-getter. He got in touch with the Horlick's Malted Milk, and he bought a little pushcart. I went with him, and he'd take and peddle this Horlick's Malted Milk to the doctors and dieticians. We went around Concord Avenue and Wellesley and all those streets around Bloor Street.

Next, my dad got on with the Dominion Messenger and Signal Company. They were a protective agency; they had ticker tapes in there, and employees would take a look at the ticker tapes for fire protection and police protection.

Anyway, my father went from one job to the next. He finally got established with *The Evening Telegram*. He stayed with *The Evening Telegram* as collector for about thirty-five years.

My dad had other jobs, too—you know, part-time. He did what he could. Apart from his steady job, he borrowed a thousand dollars from one of his brothers to go out and buy a house. My dad had got the house paid off with rent. And after that house got paid off, he got the second house and got that paid off, and so on. And so when he passed away he owned three houses outright with no mortgage and no liens and no nothing.

My pay was seven dollars and fifty cents per week.

During World War One we lived in a little cottage next to the Hillcrest Public School. I started first grade or first book when I was about eight or nine or ten years of age, and I got as far as senior third. The Ontario government had some little red uniforms with little short navy-blue pants. On the twenty-fourth of May all the boys were issued these uniforms. We had wooden guns, and in the schoolyard we used to turn right and turn left and this sort of stuff. Anyway, on the twenty-fourth of May we all gathered together and we went down to Queen's Park in a march, and we had the band and the bagpipes and the whole bit. That was a long time ago. . . .

The war was declared over, and my dad was working in the offices of *The Evening Telegram*, and my uncle worked in the mailing room where the papers come off the press. So my uncle sent me a bundle of newspapers and I went out and I got all kinds of money for the papers. People would give you a quarter for a five-cent paper. I made about ten dollars that day.

Then my father went to the board of education and made an application that I cease going to school, and I was relieved from public school in the third grade. I was just about to start on fractions, and bingo! . . .

So after that I never got back to school again. He knew a man who worked in the University of Toronto, and they found me a job. I swept the floor, filled the bottles with acid and ammonia and stuff. I did errands for the professors and the students, washed bottles and beakers, made myself generally useful. I worked from about eight in the morning until five at night. My pay was seven dollars and fifty cents per week, but we got paid every two weeks, so we'd go up to the main office and get our cheque for fifteen bucks. Fifteen bucks, I guess, was supposed to be a lot of money in those days. ✎

Little by Little, Things Stick

For many who come to Ontario from distant lands, the English language proves a lifelong challenge, beloved and frustrating. But, as this man from Georgetown found, little by little, things stick.

I was eighteen and I didn't have any English education whatsoever. I started to work right away as a busboy. With the little English I learned as a busboy I tried to read comic books, and it helped—mind you, I skipped most of the words, but I got the idea.

A year later I went to the race-track and stayed there for three years until I got a chance to be a jockey. Then things started to happen. I rode at six different race-tracks and I was champion of all six race-tracks. I guess I rode on guts alone, you know. I wanted to be somebody, let me put it that way. This was important to me, and it's still important to me today—to be successful, no matter what the effort is.

From there I went to the States and rode all over the United States from coast to coast at different race-tracks. Last year I won my four-thousandth race, and I thought to go out the right way, you know, on a high note, so I quit after four thousand wins.

I enjoyed my life up to now—fantastic! I had dreams I set out to do, and I fulfilled all my dreams. So many people have dreams, and none of them come true. All my dreams came true: it's fantastic. . . .

I came to Canada to be Canadian. My dad was the first one to take out a Canadian citizenship paper. He says, "This is where we'll stay, and this is where we'll die." It meant a lot to me because he went through two wars, and he says, "If they ever come again a third time, this is where I'm gonna stay. This is what I'm gonna do."

All my dreams came true.

I'm very proud of my dad, but he never managed the English language, and, so help me, I don't know how he got by. I look at words differently now than I used to. All of a sudden they mean something. If I can't read them, I keep trying till I can read the whole word, so I've established something for myself. I keep practising. If I'm not too tired, sometimes I sit down and keep writing the word over and over, and some of them do stick. Now I understand the difference—what the words mean, and where they come from, and what they represent. You know, like "the sun" or "this is my son": they sound the same, but they are spelled completely different. If you don't know this and you teach yourself how to read, it doesn't make much sense to you. Then all of a sudden it does make sense.

When I was a busboy I thought, "If only I could own a car." Then, "If I only could own a house." And everything I ever dreamed about, the horses got it for me. So, in my own mind, I'm very satisfied with my life until now, but now I have to do something new.

I think if I can learn a little bit, then I can improve myself and put the obstacles which are against me now away. To be a success, I am sure it will help. It will probably get me into a position where I could master a better job. Then again, if you have better jobs, you probably make better pay, too. So that's why I want to do this. I'm doing this really for myself. Little by little, things stick. ᔕ

Who Am I?

English is a second language for many of us in Ontario. We might have grown up with French, German, or Portuguese, with joual or Ojibwe, with Cantonese or Swahili. Or, like this woman from Toronto, we might have grown up using our hands to talk.

Deaf culture, like any culture, requires that you have a language. That is one of the five components of culture — that you have a language. Deaf people's language is ASL — American Sign Language. It has its own rules, its own facial expressions. It's a visual language; it requires a very strong use of the eyes.

The second aspect is values. Vision is one of the things we cherish the most. If you covered up the eyes, what would you do? We couldn't function that way — you must be able to have eye contact. Researchers asked deaf people, "Which would you prefer — to be blind or to lose your hands?" Most deaf people responded they would prefer to lose their hands — that the use of their eyes is what they cherish most.

The third aspect of culture is the rules. For example, one rule is that you maintain eye contact — that you don't break that eye contact. Or if you do, you must inform us of what it is. You would hold up your hand and say, "Hold it a minute, I'm looking over here.'' Hearing people may hear noise or a knock on the door—maybe somebody calls their name—so they break eye contact with the deaf person to look in the direction of the sound without saying before they do it that that's what is happening.

Another example of a rule is the way you get someone's attention in deaf culture—you tap them on the shoulder, but you don't want to do it too hard. Or you wave your hand, maybe off to the side. We are able to use our peripheral vision quite extensively, so if someone is waving their hand off to the side of my head, I can usually see that movement and they will get my attention.

The deaf student goes to the mainstream school . . . and becomes lost.

The next aspect would be heritage. This may include stories or information passed on from generation to generation. But you have to remember ASL is not a written language, so none of this has ever been written down. We're now beginning to use videotape. I think it's the best way for us to be able to save our language, so we videotape stories, jokes, funny events that may have happened—also maybe poems.

The last aspect, which is quite important, is self-identification: Who am I? Do I identify myself as a deaf person with a deaf culture? Did I grow up orally? Hard of hearing? What's my background? Where did I grow up? Where am I from? Sometimes there may be deaf parents, and they might not really participate with their deaf children. So where do they learn? Where do they socialize? Other people are mainstreamed and it can be quite confusing for them. If they have hearing parents, they might not learn this cultural information. The deaf student goes to the mainstream school with hearing students and becomes lost.

Sometimes someone might try to cover up the fact that they're deaf, but if you notice how they're using their eyes, it can be very obvious. A hearing person is very nonchalant about looking around, about talking to people. But if it's a deaf person, they can't do that; they have to really watch. They're cueing in more closely on the face. Maybe their speech is different. It may be a little slower, it may sound forced or stilted. Also, maybe some behaviour is different. You might notice that they tap people on the shoulder to get attention. You might see that they are always sitting in the front of the class, especially in the mainstream school. That's a must. You have to sit in the front row so that you're able to see the teacher and lip-read them clearly.

Most times if there are crowds of people, you can notice differences of behaviour if you're looking for it and know what to look for, and then you'd know that they're deaf. I think you just become more sensitive to it.

The Only Thing I Heard Was "Stupid"

Each of us has a story about our school days. Some of us remember playgrounds and friends and praise from the teacher. These people from Cornwall remember a different story.

I never really felt that I was an illiterate. Twenty years ago it really meant nothing. The only thing I heard was "stupid".

* * *

I never could learn anything, so they never gave me books.

* * *

There were so many people that when I tried to talk, they wouldn't care. And when I go home it was always negative. Like, if I'm stupid, well, I might as well be stupid.

* * *

Because I couldn't read and write I was pushed to one side. I didn't like going to school, period. I wasn't learning nothing. I said that to myself, I said, "What am I doing here? They're not doing anything here—they're just laughing."

* * *

I liked school—for a while. Until it got difficult. Then it wasn't fun anymore. I had a lot of friends, and I did enjoy my classes—my history, geography. But the English class, spelling and that, was just a nightmare. At the end I didn't like being there at all.

*   *   *

Them days, kids would laugh at you if you didn't know a word, and if you were reading and you said the word wrong, everybody would laugh.

*   *   *

I wanted to learn. But there was no help.

If you couldn't read the teacher said, "Fine. Somebody who can read, stand up."

*   *   *

I wanted to learn. *I wanted to learn.* But there was no help. They just figured, well, that's it, she's too late. The bloom's gone, as they say. I think I was just too quiet because I was just too scared of the language barrier, for one, and they didn't feel that they wanted you, for two, and there was no help.

*   *   *

At the time, my parents were separated. They didn't know much about what was going on. They knew we were going to school. They didn't know what school.

*   *   *

See, my mother never pushed me. She would say, "If you don't want to do it, don't do it." That's it. She was not a woman to push.

*   *   *

My mother signed me out because, she says, I didn't need to go to school. I didn't need the education.

*   *   *

So I just wouldn't go to school. I wouldn't go. I would make pretend like I was sick and I wouldn't go.

*   *   *

I'd lose my page, that was a good one.

*   *   *

When I knew it was my turn to read I'd go to the bathroom.

*   *   *

Or they used to say, "Well, tomorrow, you there—you'll read chapter six." So I'd skip school because it was my turn. Then I wouldn't go back to school the next day. I'd wait three or four days and then go back.

*   *   *

I've always been able to talk well, and I think that really helped me in hiding it and not letting on—not being shy, being more aggressive. If you get into a conversation with someone, and somebody's going to read to you, say, "Ah, forget this crap!" and just stare him down, or just change it. It was being aggressive, also being smart—but not smart enough to read.

Anybody's Dream

This man grew up in an institution at Smith's Falls, where kindness didn't seem to come naturally to most members of the staff. Yet, far from being bitter, he has grown into a man who believes in miracles.

I was taken away from the Children's Aid and put in an institution. That bothered me; I always wanted to know who my real parents were.

It was a very, very, big, big system. It held a lot of people. It was a very big place. It stuck out like a sore thumb—that's how big it was. A bedroom was very small. Four people were in a room. Everyone had their own nightstand.

One guy was a seizure victim. He was hit around, punched around, and slapped around. He was hit around more than I can believe. You could be as good as a cupcake and still get beat on.

Another guy was a wheelchair victim. He had sugar diabetes. He tried to stay out of trouble. If there was trouble, he would try to get clear away from it, but there were a lot of times he couldn't get out of trouble. There was just trouble looking for him.

It didn't matter how you worked the game. You could try and stay out of trouble, but it didn't always work. There would always be someone there to stir up trouble.

Some staff knew how to be nice to you and talk to you; they looked at you as human beings, not as animals or as some retard or some jerk. We talked with them, played games. We horsed around, we teased each other, we called each other names. We threw eggs at them, we threw juice and water. We would squirt them with squirt guns. It was hard to find people like that. I mean, you gotta know who you are joking with.

No arguments, or you get slapped around.

A lot of the staff didn't talk at all. They didn't care, as far as I'm concerned. They were just there for the money, and the money only: "You, go to bed! . . . You, go to bed or you go in the corner! . . . You, go in the corner!" That's it. No arguments, or you get slapped around.

I did get slapped around and I got pushed into a corner. I stood in the corner and there was nothing I could do. You could be in there from one o'clock till maybe five o'clock or six o'clock. You did what you were told and that's it—no questions asked. That's how it was. You could fight back all you want, but you would never win because nobody was there to help you. There was no good guy or bad guy: there was just tough all around.

There were times I wanted to take on the whole world because I was so frustrated. I was mad. I was angry and there was nothing I could do. So, I finally gave up and played along with them.

I used to take out my frustrations by going to the gymnasium to throw the basketball. Then I got to know other people playing wheelchair basketball. They were not living in Smiths Falls—they lived in Kingston.

He brought his whole football team down to play wheelchair basketball against us.

They would help us out just by talking to us; they would talk to us just like normal people.

I got a football helmet from Gerry Organ, one of the Ottawa Roughriders. I wrote to him and told him I lived in an institution. I said I was a fan of his and he was my favourite field-goal kicker. He came out to the Rideau Regional to see me. He gave me his autograph. He gave me the football helmet he wore to games. He introduced me to his two kids and his wife. He brought his whole football team down to play wheelchair basketball against us. I was really surprised to see the whole team come down. I think he surprised everybody. It could be anybody's dream. I didn't think a football player would take the time to come down, but he did. Seeing him was believing it. It was a miracle.

A Sobering Experience

Life is generous to most of us in Ontario. But even in a peaceful farming community like Waupoos Island, disaster can strike when we least expect it.

The first thing I recall was my mother yelling, "Jack, get up! The house is on fire!" Jack was my father. We all jumped up and there was smoke in the house already. We went through the living room and we opened the kitchen door. The whole kitchen part was just ablaze. We heard our dog barking in there and we tried to call him. He'd gotten frightened and had gone in under the stove. That was where we found him after the fire, burnt up.

It was a very cold night in February. And the part of the house that we were in, the doors had been closed up. You couldn't get out of the door—it had been nailed shut from the outside. So my sister went right out through the window. She just went through, just like that, and her and I went out through the window.

We weren't able to save anything, just lost virtually everything. I recall standing outside in the snow, in about twenty-six below, in my pyjamas and bare feet, and watching the house burn down. It was a clapboard house. The thing that sticks in my memory was standing in the cold and the snow and watching the clapboards burning and peeling off, one at a time, from down the side of the house. It was quite an experience, you know. In the morning you take stock and you find that you've got one pair of pyjamas, no toothbrush or anything else. It's a sobering experience for a kid, you know.

We stayed in the barn overnight.

So anyway, we were quite a ways from the neighbour's, and rather than try to make our way to their place in the middle of the night, we stayed in the barn overnight. In the morning Dad got up and got something—bags or something—around his feet and managed to go down to Tom Bellwood's. They came back with some clothes and took us down there. But all the neighbours were really wonderful. Country folk stick together and they help out. ∽

Thrown to the Floor and Stunned

This woman from Athens found that the memory of disaster can haunt you all your life.

On the twenty-second of May in 1919, I was at school and a very serious thunderstorm came up. And all the children had left but the teacher and I. And the lightning tore the chimney all apart, and parted, and went around both walls. The wainscotting was torn out in twenty-two places from a sliver wide to a whole board wide. And I was thrown to the floor and stunned for quite some time.

The old caretaker came in and looked and saw that the teacher was able to get around a little. After I fell I was holding the swing door open, and she thought she should get me pulled back with the storm so severe. So the old gentleman went to the next neighbour and told him that the school had been hit. The neighbour said, "Is there anybody in it?", and the caretaker said, "Oh yes, there's two in there."

So he rushed his little Ford car up and got us in and took us home. The teacher boarded at our house. I was for a few days in bed with burns, especially on my right side. My stockings was scorched on the inside, and my yellow shirt scorched on the inside, but it didn't show on the outside. My mother always kept my stockings as proof that she could show. And my shoe eyelets were blisters on both feet.

Whenever a thunderstorm would come up . . . I couldn't stay awake.

I didn't go back to school anymore that year—I was in a nervous condition. An aunt of mine was visiting our family, and she asked Mother if she could take me home with her to Dundas. And the doctor said it was the best thing that they could do for me was a complete change.

A very unusual thing: whenever a thunderstorm would come up after that, I couldn't stay awake. I was visiting at my grandmother's one day, and a thunderstorm was coming up, and Grandma wondered what she was ever going to do with me. But I just curled up on the couch in the kitchen and went sound asleep. And that was the way I was the rest of the season.

School carried on until the end of June, but I couldn't go to school anymore that year. When my aunt brought me home in time to school in September, everybody was so happy to see me looking so much better.

One day I got talking to a man who lives here in Maple View Lodge, and I asked him where he lived before he came to the Lodge. And he said he lived in Harlem School for three years. And that's the school. And he said, "You know, that school was hit with lightning one time." And he said, "A girl was hurt very badly." And I said, "Yes, and that girl was me!"

He Was a Dandy

Some disasters come out of nowhere to strike a family or a town. Others, like the Depression of the thirties, are made by people and hit everyone. This man from St. Marys remembers how his boss fought the Depression with compassion.

My boss, Mr. Lind, there was nobody like him. He was the grandest man I've ever seen. He was good to everybody.

In the Depression time, 1930, he called me in one day and said, "I've got a job for you to do." I thought to myself, "I've got a job!" He said, "Sit down, I want to talk to you about it." So I sat down, and he said, "Now that we're only working part-time, I want you to go around and interview all the men that are laid off work." I said, "Boy, that's going to be some job!" I said that to myself.

When he got through talking to me I said, "Mr. Lind, just what questions should I ask these people?" He said, "The first thing I want to know is how their credit is downtown." I said, "Oh boy, if that ain't a . . ." and he said, "I want to know how many children they've got and how much rent they pay." And he said, "Remember, you can tell these people that it's only between them, you, and I. Nobody else knows anything about what's going on."

So I started out and I went to one fellow and I went to the door and I said, "Can I see you and Missus?" He said, "Yes, come on in." So I went in and I said, "Send the children into the front part of the house. I've got some things to say to you, and I'm going to ask you some very embarrassing questions. If you don't want to answer them, you say no." And I said, "I have to tell you this: if you say no to me once, you won't get a chance to say it again because I won't be back."

"My credit downtown is not worth a damn."

He looked at his wife, they kind of smiled, and he said, "Let's hear what you have to say." So I said, "How's your credit downtown?" He looked at her and said, "Not worth a damn." He made pretty good money, and he says, "My credit downtown is not worth a damn." I said, "All right. How many children do you have?" He said, "We've got two." I asked him about his rent, and he told me that, and I asked him a few more questions. I was making a note of them. I had a notebook. So I took it all down and I said, "I'll be back to see you in a couple of days to see how you're getting along." I said, "Remember, this is between you and I and Mr. Lind."

And that's the way I spent the Depression. After all this Depression was over, Mr. Lind had a big party—before they started back to work they had a big party. We had about half a dozen ice cream cars from Stratford, and he had all the families and everything. And then he got up—he wasn't any speaker, but we had a big stone outside, and he got up there and he said, "Well, boys or men, we're going back to work on full-time on Monday morning, and I hope you're getting back, and we all get back, and there will be an increase in the wages."

So after there was work for two or three weeks, he called me in one afternoon and he said, "Have you got everything about the people?" And I said, "Yes." He said, "Well, anybody that got any money from here or got coal or wood, the coal and the wood is free, gratis, and they can have that, and they can give you fifty cents a pay or a dollar a pay or whatever they can afford, and if they can't, they don't have to give us anything." He was a wonderful man. He was a dandy.

All a Rat

This woman from Kingston remembers the terrible disasters of World War II. She wondered at the time and she wonders today if we really knew what was going on.

We used to listen to the news all the time. They would always be telling how the Allies were bombing Germany, and the planes were sent down. Oh, there were maybe fifteen German planes shot down that night, and only maybe two of the Allies. I said to myself, "If we are that smart, this war should be over! Why is it taking so long? We lose two and we shoot down fifteen!" But you can't say anything, you know, because the war is on.

You know Gordon Sinclair? He was the radio announcer at that time. He was fed this stuff, and of course that was his job—to broadcast that to us. He was on TV after the war. You know Front Page Challenge? This question was brought up, and he said, "You mean to tell me that was propaganda I was broadcasting?" And the man said, "Yes. Didn't you know that?" And Gordon Sinclair—he didn't know it! Well, now, stupid me—a woman—could tell the difference. Why couldn't *he* tell the difference? The

Allies were so smart, and yet the war lasted that length of time. To this day I still swear that this is all a rat.

Another thing, when you mention about the war. The U.S. didn't come into the war until long after. I remember the day. It was on the first day of September 1939, when Germany declared war on England, and the third day of September England declared war on Germany. The tenth day of September 1939, Canada entered the war. But the United States didn't enter the war until later, I think.

And the poor Russians—they talk now about the Russians— but I felt terribly sorry for the Russian people. I remember seeing it on the shows, and it came on the radio, too. They weren't prepared for war; they didn't have the clothes to wear. They'd walk maybe in six-foot snow with a heavy gun, and not properly dressed, and they perished. They weren't treated properly, not like a human being. But they used to say, "Ah, they are only Russians." I'm not a Russian—I'm of Scottish descent—but I thought it was very, very mean.

But I say the whole thing, to my way of thinking, was all a racket. They were pushed into it. Even though they might have thought that I was just a stupid woman, I still say it was all a racket. I saw it right on television. Gordon Sinclair said, "You mean to tell me I was broadcasting propaganda?" And the man said, "Yes, you were!" ৶

A Woman Was Really a Slave

Boom times or bust, wartime or peacetime, farmers have to get the chores done and the crops in. On a farm in Palmer Rapids, life was a constant battle with time and the weather.

I've been a housewife all my life, a farmer—I drove horses and did everything, only I didn't learn how to drive a car. I got balky. I wouldn't drive the tractor because I had always had to drive the horses. August would come in and have his dinner and then he'd go and lie down and have a rest and he'd say, ''Now you go out and hitch up the horses.''

So I'd go and hitch up the horses and I had pulled out into the field and did some of the work before he'd come out! Then he'd be working hard and working late and so forth and so on, you know—you had to have a little sympathy for him. But I was working all the time, too. I'd come in and get the meal while he sat down and rested, then he rested after the meal while I did the dishes.

Awoman was really a slave! That is about it!

I pitched hay and piled it in the loft. That little loft used to get full, and *hot*! And a man shoving them big bundles in there to you and blocking the hole, you know, so you couldn't even get a breath of fresh air. . . . Yep! I did all that! I picked stones, I seeded, I disked, I harrowed—but I didn't plow. I never plowed and I never drove a tractor. Otherwise, I think I did everything on the farm, even to castrating the little pigs.

A Cruel Job

Today few people would be inclined to see tobacco as a blessing, but in the early 1930s it was a boon for Norfolk County. However, even then prosperity had its darker side, as this man's story shows.

When I was nine years old, tobacco came to Norfolk County. It's a very sandy area. I can remember the sand blowing across 24 Highway, just like snowdrifts. It was a semi-desert until Forestry took over, and the Forestry Farm started up. The government encouraged farmers to plant trees as windbreaks to control wind erosion and increase water retention in the soil.

With the coming of tobacco, farmers were starting to make a fair living. They took better care of their soil, planted cover crops and windbreaks. Tobacco really was a saviour for Norfolk County.

I got a dollar-fifty a day working for German share growers when I was nine years old because I was used to driving horses. Others were getting a dollar a day. I drove the horses on the tobacco boats. We'd have a single horse in front of the boat and we'd go between the rows. They'd pick the leaves, starting with the sand leaves, then the seconds and thirds, and all the way up the stalk

as the leaves ripened in the fall. They'd place these leaves in the boat by the armfuls.

My job was to drive the horses back and forth from the kiln to the field. On that particular farm the horses weren't too good and they weren't big enough for the job. It was a cruel job. I was told I had to run the horses all the way back after hauling those boats all the way up to the kiln. Then, I'd have to put the lines to the horses and get back there to take the next boat. I was used to looking after good horses and not misusing them. It really bothered me, but a job was a job in those days.

Each year you'd read in the paper about horses dropping dead of sunstroke in the fields, from misuse. A lot of those farmers would tie their horses up to the fence and go in to dinner, never giving the horse a drink of water. My boss would never do that, but the horses weren't too good.

One farm where I helped to get the tobacco off before the fall had such beautiful horses! They'd run back to the barn after a day's work. One particular horse was about as big as a race horse. He was coming up the lane and he just couldn't go any further. The kiln boss, Little Mike, was so upset that he got on its back and beat the horse with the traces, but the horse was just too small for the work. Finally my sister, who was about seventeen or eighteen, came over and said, "Mike, if you hit that horse once more, we're all going to quit." He stopped! ✍

How to Play the Day

In bygone days most little towns had a barbershop and a blacksmith, a general store and a church or two, a school and a hotel. And almost every town had a special little industry tended by proud and skilful workers, like this cheesemaker from Lyndhurst.

I learned the trade of cheese making at Pembroke, and I will give you a recipe as to how to play the day in the cheese factory.

At 6:00 a.m., enter factory, light the fire in boiler room to get steam up. Prepare your vats for milk, with conductor and strainers. We turn all the cheese in the curing room every morning. Look at fire in the boiler room, then go to breakfast.

Back again to take milk in to weigh it and to take a sample to be tested for butterfat, as that is the way patrons were paid for their milk. You have to have a good smeller, too, so as not to get some milk that is not desirable.

We put a culture into the vat. This we called a starter. About eight gallons. We boiled this milk and put it through a pasteurization from about eight o'clock and close it off around twelve. And it has to be cold—place in cold water. And at the end of the day we put a pint of culture in. And in the morning it is ready to use the next day.

Then we measure out some rennet—three ounces to one thousand pounds of milk. Then wait until it is set, probably twenty minutes. Then cut with a knife: the length way of that, then change your knife. Then you have to go across the vat this last time. Then you use a rake. Then you are cooking curds slowly to at least 102 degrees. It makes. By stirring the curds and getting rid of the moisture, your curds firm up nicely. You keep piling curds up, and curds will go into a solid chunk. Then you use a knife and cut and double up.

About three o'clock, curds should be ready to mill. You fork it over to air it out and keep it level. Let set for fifteen to eighteen minutes, and then fork again. This happens many times before it is ready to salt. Then you set it again for fifteen to eighteen minutes, then fork it again. Keep warm. Do not let curds get greasy. When it shrinks a bit, nice and smooth, and you can pull it like a piece of elastic, it will strip right up. Let it set for fifteen minutes. In the meantime, get ready to put the curds into the press. Be ready to press again.

You may have to return to tighten press at different intervals before retiring. Take cheese out of hoops next day after noon meal. And in the curing room they go.

"M28"

When the war came, great numbers of women were hired to work in huge, noisy, high-pressure factories, like Canada Locomotive in Kingston. Women like this one were given important responsibilities and experienced a new pride and power.

I worked for the Canadian Locomotive Company from late '41 or early '42. What we did was to take the big racer plates that were on the bottom of the naval guns and manoeuvre them down into place. These are big things—the ones that turn the naval guns around. They went on a hub in the centre, and I had to put them on properly because we worked precision work and a thou made an awful difference.

The broach was a stainless steel, high-tempered thing that went in through the hole with a round piece, and you made it secure. It was cooled by oil running constantly on it. You couldn't let it bounce because you would lose again your thousandth. It had to run absolutely smooth through, and as it went through—once the hole went through—it was no longer round; it was an oblong hole. And this was with one straight, steady bite.

From the broaching machine I was very, very interested in all sorts of things that were going on, so I went on a training course around the shops. There I learned the horizontal grinder. I learned how to make nuts and bolts with a bicycle lathe. I learned the milling machine. From there I learned to read blueprints, and from that I was asked if I would like to go on an inspection team. So that's where I went. I worked up until I was given my very own work mark, which was "M28". I will always remember the number. The way they explained it was that "M28" was my number, and it would be mine forever and ever and ever. Nobody would ever get that number.

I didn't even know there was rifling in the barrel of a gun.

I inspected everything. I finished my very last inspection just as the naval gun was mounted and the armour plate was on. I had to take a fish scale and I had to be able to turn that complete naval gun around a full circle with less than a ten pound on the fish scale, and then I had to be able to raise it and lower it by just turning my finger. These were the guns that sit right on the front of the corvette. They weren't tested as to firing, but we had to test the rifling inside the barrel. I didn't even know there was rifling in the barrel of a gun till I learned all of these things.

And then they would bring the big flat bed with the train right into the shop, and we would oil the gun down and they would crate it. I would stand there for all the time that this was going on. When we finally put the strapping around it and we put the seal on it, then my "M28" went on that, too. It went on every gun we made.

My dad was trained in the Canadian Locomotive Company as a boy and pensioned off from the Canadian Locomotive Company. But that is one of the humorous things. No matter how you spell it, most of the chaps in the top positions worked on piecework; what *we* were doing was all precision work. And precision work and piecework just can't mix. If they could put it over us they would, which made us even more determined to do our job right.

I had turned down . . . one too many.

I had a father and two uncles working in there, and when I was at work with my overalls on, they weren't even my relatives; they were working the same as everyone else. My one uncle—his job was putting the armour plate on the naval guns—and I can remember so clearly, I had turned down about four of his guns in quick time and he almost hated me. He might have spent eight hours working on something that I would throw out in two minutes flat, and he would have to strip it and redo it.

The one particular time that stands out in my mind so clearly is that I had turned down just obviously one too many, and he hit the roof. It was on Armistice Day, and I had said to him, "This one has got to be stripped," and I turned around and walked away. At that particular time it came eleven o'clock, and they blew the whistle for a two-minute silence. I don't think my uncle in his temper even heard the whistle because through his two-minute silence he started banging the armour plate. They had to go down and get him and take him out.

But I had to have pride in my work because, as I explained before, they gave me my work mark—"M28". They told me that mark is me on those guns and that if I was proud enough to put my work mark on it, then it had to be like me. And I am like that —when I do something, I do it all the way or I don't do it at all.

As Unconcerned As Nothing

It takes a special kind of calm to help people in pain. One nurse from Kingston was so good at keeping her feelings in check that she ran the risk of being misunderstood.

I had . . . let me see . . . one, two, three deaths that I can recall offhand from injuries.

One man, Ab, who was strong as a bull, came to the door after I had got a new floor from the manager. And he said, "Every *!*!*! man in the yard ought to take off their hat to you— you got that new floor!" I said, "Come on in." "No," he said, "I never was sick a day in my life." And away he went.

Just after lunch I heard this racket and all of a sudden they said, "Come quick, Nurse!" I went over and Ab was lying on the boiler. The boiler broke and he swallowed all that steam and his hips were cooked.

So I phoned Doctor Twiddle. "We are having a massive burn case come in. I think he will require surgery and his hand is just hanging," I said. "Where the hell is he?" he asks. "He is in the dry dock, jammed in a crane, and we are trying to get him out."

It was a very precarious position for the rest of us because one move and the thing would come down and kill us all.

It was quarter to five when we got him out of there. I had been giving hypos on him. I said, "Dr. Twiddle, you are only wasting drugs," I said, "you might as well be injecting a roast of beef because he is cooked."

He lived for about two weeks.

So when we got him out I went with him to the operating room. Ab said, "Will I be all right, Nurse?" I said, "Sure you will, Abner, you told me how strong you are." "That's right," he said. "But what about my left hand? They are going to be able to save that? 'Cause, you know, that's my fiddle hand." 'Cause he played the fiddle. I said, "Well, I guess it will last as long as you will, Ab."

He lived for about two weeks. He never blacked out, but when he'd breathe, it would be just like when you see kids with bubble gum—but in his nose.

Then there was another lad from the Island—Ambrose. He was working down under the bridge. He had never worked on a boat in his life. He burned a hole and then he stepped back in it. He slid down about twenty-eight feet and landed on an angle bar. He was split from the eye to over the ear. When they got him out, his brains were hanging out. He lived from Friday morning until Tuesday morning.

And another man—what was his name? . . . He was down working under the big overhead crane. There was a fellow up in the crane, and he didn't know the other one was down there working and he released it. It fell on him and it crushed him up against the cement. He was just smushed like a fly. The men were vomiting and going on. I just went down and I looked at him, eh. I came back and I phoned the undertaker and I said, "Come down." I said, "Don't bring anything fancy because it's a messy, messy job. Bring your rubber sheeting to protect your stretcher." So I picked up his tongue from one place and his arm from another.

I was talking to the undertaker about six months after and I said, "I suppose you get some messy jobs in here, eh?" He said, "Yes, the worst mess I ever got was the place they call the shipyards. There was that nurse walking around picking up fingers and hands and ears and legs. You'd think she was collecting chips to make a fire," he said. "She was just as unconcerned as nothing." I started to laugh.

Just Gas

Bravery comes in many guises and it isn't always glamorous. In this story from Killaloe, a young woman's spunk transforms what could have been an ordeal into a simple case of waiting and hoping for the best.

My first child was delivered by my mother-in-law. The doctor was here for the second one, but my mother-in-law did all the work for the first. I was definitely doing natural childbirth that they make such a fuss about these days. I thought it was fun.

There was little ups and downs, but I didn't go to bed and just lay there waiting for a pain to come. I walked around, then I'd feel my back hurting a little bit extra and I'd hit the rocking chair and I'd drop and just rock and rock and rock. Then I'd get up and walk around a little bit in the kitchen again.

This all started about nine o'clock in the evening. Because we had cabbage for supper and I had eat quite a bit, I thought it was just the gas from the cabbage. So we went ahead to bed—put out the lamps and went to bed. It kept getting worse and worse and I said, "Darn that cabbage!" But it kept on till my husband said,

"It wouldn't be time for the baby?" And I said, "No, Doctor said it was September it was due to be born."

But two o'clock came and I wasn't any smarter. I was really walking around then. Back in those days, though we didn't buy medication, we used some old home remedies. So I put a little water in a glass and some vinegar, sugar, and a little drop of soda. Makes a fizz. I drank that to try and get the gas off. I'm nineteen, and I still thought it was gas!

But two o'clock came and I wasn't any smarter.

Anyway, when four o'clock came, my husband said, "I'm not going to wait any longer, I'm going to get Ma." He went over, and his mother came back and she said, "Get some water on quick, we haven't got time to waste!" So it didn't take long. He held the lamp and she delivered the baby. The baby was born around six o'clock in the morning. One long night. . . .

The Cat Got It!

We often discover reserves of bravery that we never suspected we had. This woman from Palmer Rapids did what she had to do to relieve a neighbour's pain.

Mr. Brodofski—old Grandpa Brodofski—he got a sore finger. It was all swelled up and yellow, and Billy brought him up with the horses and buggy, and he wanted me to lance it. So I borrowed a needle—a sewing needle—and I ripped it open and the pus just come . . . I don't know . . . it was terrible! He'd been up all night walking like this with his hand up with the pain. Then I bandaged it.

Billy brought him up every morning for me to dress that finger. They were digging potatoes—it was in the fall—and I made a finger out of deerskin for him to cover it so that he wouldn't get sand in it. It was for a couple of weeks I had to do that.

One morning he come up, and this bone had rotted off and it was sticking out through this hole that was here—part of the bone. I took my tweezers and I went to pull it out. Edna was with him, and he says, "Hell, hell! Hell! Hell! Hell!"—that's all he could say in English. And Edna says to me, "Don't hurt my grandpa!" So I said, "I'll take you to Combermere to the doctor." He says, "No, no! No! No! No!" So I tried it once again; I put my tweezers on it and I jerked it out—it came out! It came right out! And I had that bone and I was going to keep it for the rest of my life, but I left it on the cookhouse table one night and the cat got it! ∽

For Reasons of Taste and Pride

Some industries, like the stoneworks of St. Marys, bloom out of the earth of the town itself.

The two big quarries that we have now—one is the swimming quarry and the other is the water reservoir—originally were a whole series of individual quarries. Local stone masons would own one of these quarries, from which they would quarry the stone. They'd quarry it off during the winter and shape it. Then in the summer, when they did the building, they had the stone on hand.

The stone, as you know if you've ever walked along the river, is in layers. It's very smooth—it's like walking on a kind of hard carpet. What a quarryman would do would be to take a great crowbar and cut the stone out in big pieces. It would come out in layers, and the thickest layer might be eight or ten or fourteen inch. That would be the most valuable, and those thick layers are used as sills and lintels in buildings all around town.

The great age of stone construction was in the 1850s and the 1860s. In 1851, there were five or six stone houses in St. Marys.

By the 1860s there were several dozen. Then brick became popular, and the 1870s and 1880s are a period of brick construction. Then, with the Town Hall in 1891, the library in 1904, the Opera House back in '78-'79, we have important stone buildings again.

With a well-directed blow he would cut the piece of stone out.

When the stones were taken out of the quarries they were in layers. Then the stone mason would take his chisel and with a well-directed blow he would cut the piece of stone out, and then here you have the front that's going to face out from the building. Now he could do one of two things. He could smooth off that stone, and then what you had was what we call a ''smooth-face facade'' to your building. Or he can decide that he will dress it in a rough-faced way: he would take his chisel and chop it like this and chop it like that, so the front would be sort of pointed in what is called a ''hammered rest'', or ''rock face'', or ''rough-faced front''. The second technique was more common around the turn of the century, and the first technique was more common in the 1860s.

An excellent example is the old post office. *There* was a very prominent building, and the government and the municipality said, ''We're going to have a new post office, and it's going to be an imposing building. It's going to be big and it's going to have a rough-face front. It's not only going to have limestone, but it's going to have that sort of red sandstone through it. It's going to be two and a half to three stories high, with an elaborate roof structure.'' And they decided, consciously and for reasons of taste and pride, that their style of construction was going to make it a building that people would stop and look at—as they do even today.

Balm of Gilead

The power of healing is one of the great gifts people offer one another. It requires not only compassion, but endless study of nature's gifts. Let this man from Sharbot Lake tell you about a sovereign remedy.

Balm of Gilead salve. It's the best cure for any wounds that was ever in the country. They make it out of deer tallow and Balm of Gilead buds. The trees have a big bud on them and it's full of . . . like resinous stuff . . . stick to your fingers. And the thing is to know how to get that material, that gum out of it. You have to have deer's tallow—render the deer's tallow that comes off the deer hide, eh? I have it setting by now for this spring.

Look here, you can cure anything. I came from the hospital in Ottawa and I was bedridden for half the winter, so much my tailbone got a blister on it, and they doctored for three weeks nearly. So these people were here, and the nurses were in doctoring. The Scot put a bandage on it and doctored it pretty nearly every day. If anything, it was getting worse. I couldn't hardly lay on my back.

So I happened to say to them, "Good God, if I had some Balm of Gilead salve, I'd cure that." But they didn't know what I was talking about, and where do you get it, and what. "Well," I said, "it's an Indian medicine. My mother used to make it, and I know how to make it. But I don't know where you'd get it at this time of the year."

Just a little bit of that stuff will . . . cure anything.

And they went and phoned around to different places up here and, by gosh, if they didn't come up with the Balm of Gilead salve! Do you know something—and you could verify it—three applications and away went this thing. Never came back! That's Balm of Gilead salve. That's the real McCoy there, if you want to cure any bad sores or anything. The old people called it "Balm of Gileah", but the right book name for it is "Balm o' Gilead", according to the lumber books that I've got.

"**B**alm o' Gilead"! . . . Well, that's the choice medicine. If you cut yourself and had a bad wound, and a doctor having an awful time trying—you put a dab of that on and see what'll happen. It'll clear it right up!

I didn't get a deer last fall, but buddies that I was huntin' with they all got a deer. We got the tallow off it, just exactly off of the hide where we wanted it, to make the medicine. A little—just a little bit of that stuff will make a lot of medicine. Cure anything.

This deer tallow come right off the deer's hide. Down near where the tail is, you know, just up from that about five or six inches, there's flakes of this tallow. It's the real McCoy! There's inside tallow, too, but it's not as special as this stuff that's on the outside of the hide. You see, being that the deer ate all the herbs and roots and vegetation, put it with this Balm of Gilead, and this is the makeup of this Indian cure.

You can just wipe a little on your finger. You'd think it was greasy, but it's tallow. And damned if you can get that gum out of the bud with anything else. Well, you can get it out with a grease of some kind, but it's not as medicinal as the deer tallow—that's the McCoy. The deer tallow has to come, or it wouldn't be as good a medicine. *That* is special.

Faster Than a Horse

Before the days of TV, people were more ready to devise their own entertainment and to enter into the spirit of things. In this story from Sharbot Lake, the whole neighbourhood turns out to watch a man race against a horse.

Dad could run. Of course, people did walk and run in those days. And talking about running, they used to laugh about the time my father beat his uncle, Jack McKinnon, who was in McDonald's Corners with his horse.

He had bought a racehorse, and he was blowing about this racehorse being so good. And Dad bet him that he could beat the racehorse in a race. And so he took up the bet. And of course everybody in a place like McDonald's Corners—the whole neighbourhood—was out.

Dad knew that you could run faster than a horse on a long run, you see. On a short run you couldn't, but on a long run. A person who can run, that is.

So it was from McDonald's Corners to our place, you see— eight miles. He had the horse on a buggy, you see, and Dad gave him, they said, a hundred yards ahead.

And they started to run. Of course now they've put in the new road, but there used to be a very large hill right about four miles from McDonald's Corners—right near Paul's Creek. There was a very large hill, and on the hill Dad passed him, going up the hill. And then he was ahead from then on, and he got home. He was home in time, and he went to the spring and got a pail of water, and he was coming back with the pail of water when Jack McKinnon drove in with the horse.

Sometimes They Sing Another Song

Imagine a week of feasting and singing, followed by a horse-and-buggy honeymoon! A hundred years ago? Well, yes, it could have been, but then it could also be today—because this is a story from a Mennonite community near Chatham.

First you go on the Sunday evening and ask to be married. Then you got to wait till Saturday till you have the wedding. They write the names—who are the ones—and so they got a week to send the letters around to invite the people who they want to have them come. And then Saturday, ten o'clock it starts until ten o'clock at night.

Usually they get married where the girl belongs to. People start coming and shaking hands and sometimes at the same time they bring you presents or whatever. And then they have a dinner. And then after dinner they sing a couple of songs—like for the wedding day. When that's over they start getting ready again for having a coffee break. So they have the buns and sugar—pieces of sugar. Some of them have cookies or butter for the buns. That's at 3:30 or something like that. After the coffee break they sing another song and then everybody goes home. If there is enough left over for supper—from the soup and the meat and everything—then the people that want to come, well, they got a chance. So they get together again about six o'clock or something like that—seven maybe. And sometimes they sing another song and sometimes they don't, and then that's it.

So then when the Saturday is over, then comes Sunday morning.

She has to walk behind you, that they know you're the man and she's the wife.

Sunday morning you have to go to church in the morning, and then for dinner you go to what would be my parents if I would marry her. Then we get dinner and coffee break there. Then we would go and start visiting people till about ten o'clock, and then I bring her home and I go home.

Well, then they get my buggy and horse ready, and I go and pick her up and start driving around and go to visit our relatives or our friends, you know. And then all week like that.

Then Saturday, you have to go to the people who take care of the church and ask them if they want to put chairs in the church for you to sit on in front of the counter. And so they have it ready there on the next Sunday. You come to church so you can go in, but then you wait till the church starts, and then you walk in and sit down. Then when everything is over, the preacher comes and gives you the hand and asks if you want to keep her for your wife. You have to say yes. And same to her. Then, when everything was over, they sing a song, and then, when the song has started, you walk out. And she has to walk behind you, that they know you're the man and she's the wife. But then, what you want to do, that's up to you, I guess. ∽

The Great Days of Motoring

Did people have more fun in the old days? Or is that a trick of memory? This story takes us back to the early days of the motor car, when driving was still an adventure requiring imagination and resourcefulness.

My father bought a car, a Russell Knight it was called, made by the Canada Cycle people that owned the Canada Cycle Motor Company. It was quite a car.

We'd go out in this car and it would be sailing along and you'd get a bad bump and all of a sudden the car would come to a complete stop. The chauffeur had to climb over the side and go down underneath where there was a tap that turned on the gas. It was gravity feeded and, as soon as you were through driving the car, you had to go down underneath and turn off the tap. So that was car number one.

Then we bought a Buick. The Buick had a self-starter on it—it was more modern. The other one looked more like a buggy than it looked like a car; the Buick did look like a car. It was fine until you got about a third of a tank of gas and you'd go up a hill, and she'd stall. You had to go down the hill again, turn around, and back up the hill until you got to the other side, then turn around and go on the straight again. The intake was at the wrong end of the tank.

Two or three times we went on drives and had flat tires. We'd go on safaris from Georgetown as far as Burlington and Guelph. It was a big deal!

We had to stop on the side of the road . . . and stuff the tires with the hay.

Fifteen miles an hour—that was my father's speed limit; he wouldn't let the chauffeur drive any faster than fifteen miles an hour. Of course he wouldn't be watching the thing all the time, and the chauffeur would get it up to twenty-five. Then my father would realize we were going a little too fast for him, and we had to slow down again. Those were the days. . . .

We always had flat tires. We had to stop on the side of the road and go out and get hay out of the fields and stuff the tires with the hay, to get home.

The old car, the Russell Knight, had a Gabriel Horn. It was a horn that runs off the exhaust pipe; it had a valve. This thing went blaring away like a steamship whistle—beautiful-sounding thing, like a Mississippi River boat. I was on board one day, and we came down Trafalgar Road, just ready to make the turn across to Georgetown, and a pig ran out and it got hit by the car and wedged the valve on the Gabriel Horn and blew all the tires out on

both sides. We didn't hurt the pig—*he* ran away. Then we came down the Main Street with the Gabriel Horn going right out! . . . Couldn't stop it. And both wheels on the left side stuck with straw. . . .

These were some of the great days of motoring. ဢ

"Kick the Can"

Some people have no trouble recalling the good times. Others—like this man from Sault Ste. Marie—have to look hard to find any fun moments in their past.

I spent my childhood at home in Sault Ste. Marie. I had six brothers and six sisters. And now the thing is, my mother had two sets of twins, and the thing is they died before . . . put it this way . . . they died before they were born.

My father was part French and part Indian; therefore he could talk both languages. But he spoke English at home. He didn't teach us how to talk either French or Indian. My mother spoke English. My father came from Garden River. My mother came from Sugar Island. On my father's side, I didn't know them. On my mother's side, there was her mother and her dad and three or four brothers. They lived on the island—Sugar Island.

Every second Sunday we would go over to Sugar Island to visit. My grandparents had a boat. We would ride down, and somebody would yell, "Come and get us!" And when they heard us hollering they would come over and get us. They had to make two trips.

The kids used to like to swim, but I didn't. I used to just sit there and watch them. You want to know why that is? When I was standing by the water someone would come up behind me and hit my feet and arms and throw me in. I haven't been in the water since.

As for me having fun, I never did. No, I mean I had fun once, a long time ago, many years since, let me see now . . . I just forget how many years was that. Playing "Kick the Can".

A Little Bit Better Than Before

More than a million people in Ontario have trouble reading and writing. And there are probably more than a million good reasons why some of us missed getting these skills. But there is no reason why we can't start now, even if we decide to go very slowly, like this man from Toronto.

I came from Portugal in 1953. I go near Niagara Falls on peach farm, fruit. I stay there from July to September, then the farmers don't need guys anymore. So I came to Toronto to find a job.

I found job in El Mocambo Tavern. I work in El Mocambo about six weeks. October twenty-first I went to Doctor Ballard dog-food factory, asked for job. Then Ballard sell the business to Standard Brands. Then Standard Brands sell to Nabisco. Altogether for this company I work thirty-two years.

I have tried before to go to school to learn something, but it's very difficult for me because I was in three shifts all the time. In 1985 I was thinking to go to school to learn something—to write and read. 1986, I try to go, but it was a little hard for me. And in

'87 I went to Portugal for five months. Then I think in my mind, I said, ''Man, I should go back to school.'' But I had operation—I had gallstone.

So this year in January I think, ''I'm going to school.'' So I go into school. What I think: I say it's not too late for learn if you want to learn. You no learn in one—you learn in two. Anyway, I know a little bit better than before. See, I know little bit better than before.

I say it's not too late for learn if you want to learn.

Things are like that, you know—life. My age—I'm not young, I'm over seventy now. But oh, I try. There's life, you know. Today you're alive, tomorrow you're dead. Things are like that. You worry too much, you think too much—it's no good.

When I came to Toronto you didn't find nothing what you find today. Up to Lawrence Avenue is sheep farm, goats farm. No building, nothing there. University Avenue, there's small houses, nothing what you see now. When I came, in '53, '54, '56, I used to go on Toronto Islands. There was a farm. It's like mosquitoes all over. You go there now, there's one new city. Oh, my God, it's a new city now!

But that time was more trust, people no take things like now. I used to walk on Queen Street, sometimes one o'clock in the morning, twelve o'clock in the morning, five o'clock in the morning—any hour of the night. You see in the stores, you see packs of cigarettes, you see bread, you see everything there—nobody touch. Newspapers—you have the money there, you take newspaper, you put the change. Nobody touch the money. Today you cannot do that, my friend.

I enjoy life. I still in school, I back in school. I want to go. I don't mind because I have to read. I feel I can do this, I go ahead. Take me another two years, three. I go ahead if God give . . . because I like it, you know.　ဢ

Is Anything Going to Happen Good to Me Today?

Our stories are exciting because they are unfinished. Each of us spins out a story every day from our imagination and our courage. Like this woman in Orillia who woke up one morning and asked herself a question.

I came to Orillia to work when I was about fifteen. I came from Machedash Township, where I was raised. Machedash was country roads and bush.

Where I came from was farmland. We have a river out home called the Laughlin Falls. There was twelve in our family—seven boys and five girls. We'd take a loaf of bread and some butter, and we'd go to our falls and we'd fish and cook the fish right there. And there was watercress, leeks, and everything you'd ever want.

Grandaddy was a farmer, and he sure looked like Stephen Leacock. He took his hat off and scratched his head like him, too. And he was a tall man. He lived till a hundred and one. He walked into town—ten miles from our place—every other day. And he farmed all his life, too.

I didn't go to school; I worked on the farm with him. I drove horses on the hay fork, I drove the tractor, and things like that. Then when I was fifteen I was gone. With no school, I found it hard to get a job. When I went to put an application in, I went into the office and I asked them who would be my boss. And he filled in my application for me, and that was it.

How I got in with the Literacy Centre was this: I was getting up and I was getting dressed and I said, "Please, Lord, is anything going to happen good to me today? I hope so!"

I *never* come down West Street.

So in the meantime I got dressed and I was walking down West Street. I *never* come down West Street; I generally come down Peter. So I come down West Street and I turned at the corner. And all at once I come to the Literacy Centre. I stopped and I said, "You're trying to tell me that's the Literacy Centre where you learn to read and write! Yeah, right! Thanks!"

You'll think I'm crazy. Anyway, I come in. Of course Jo-Ann knew me for years, and she says to me, "What brought you in here?" And I said to her, "I need you more than you'll ever know." She said, "Yeah?" and I said, "Yeah, because I never went to school." She said, "You never went to school?" I said, "No." So we hugged each other, and Claudia said, "You didn't?

Gee!'' So we got up and hugged each other. So Jo-Ann said, ''Can I be her teacher?'' Claudia said, ''Sure you can if you want.'' So Jo-Ann became my teacher.

I've come a long way since. Jo-Ann was a really terrific, fantastic teacher. We started right from the bottom and she learned me everything. I write letters to my twin in Toronto. I've read the Bible through, and I got my certificate for reading the Bible through. I'm going to be a Sunday school teacher after I leave here.

So I'm going to end my story. The bottom line is: Anybody that's got no education, just get out and come to the Literacy Centre. Put everything you have in it and you'll succeed—that's for sure!

Notes

The stories included in this book were chosen from hundreds told by people from across Ontario. All the stories were collected during International Literacy Year, 1990, often as a project of a local literacy program.

In most cases, the stories were recorded on audiotape, then transcribed and edited by members of local literacy or oral history programs before being submitted for inclusion in this anthology.

The notes that follow were prepared to give interested readers some background information on the stories. Each note gives the name of the program under which the work was carried out and, when the information was made available, the names of the storyteller and the collector and a brief comment on some aspect of the program. In some instances, only first names are used, in keeping with the wishes of the participants.

For more information about the stories or about the oral history projects, readers are invited to write directly to the group concerned (the address is given at the end of each note).

The Head of the Clan

This story was collected as part of the oral history project of the West Bay First Nation and submitted in a report prepared by Justeen Debassige. "The objective of the project was to seek as much information as possible on the clan groupings and outline family trees for the community of West Bay. Family names would be researched and matched with traditional and Ojibwe names, in attempts to find the clans to which these families belonged." West Bay First Nation, Excelsior P.O. Box 296, West Bay, Ontario, P0P 1G0.

There Was a Witch

This story was told by Sarah Lavalley to Diane Nicholls, a participant in the literacy program of the Community Resource Centre in Killaloe. The co-ordinators of the centre's oral history project were Kathlyn Lampi and Joanne Service. The project focused on pioneer women in Southwestern Renfrew County. "I love doing this, especially when it is easy to get the ladies to tell their stories." Community Resource Centre, P.O. Box 59, Killaloe, Ontario, K0J 2A0.

Respect for the Moose

This story was told by Joseph Ketchegesick to George Kenny of the Thunder Bay Indian Friendship Centre. "Booshoo." Thunder Bay Indian Friendship Centre, 401 North Cumberland Street, Thunder Bay, Ontario, P2A 4P7.

What Started the Fuss

This story was told by Lawrence Sherbert to members of the Manomin Keezis Aboriginal Peoples Alliance. The group's oral history project was compiled and edited by Carol Pepper and Jennifer Tsun: "We represent Métis and off-reserve Native people in the Sharbot Lake area. We will be looking at many different aspects of how Native people in our area lived." The literacy program of the Manomin Keezis Aboriginal Peoples Alliance is no longer in operation.

Slowly Surfacing

This story was told by Lisa, a former ESL student, to Penny Jensen and other ESL students at the Dryden Literacy Association. "Lisa was first involved with the Dryden Literacy Association as an ESL student, then as a member of the board of the association for the past seven years. She has tutored many students." Dryden Literacy Association, 23A King Street, Dryden, Ontario, P8N 1B4.

My Father Was a Go-Getter

This story was told by William Major to members of the YMCA Literacy Program of Toronto. Catherine O'Brien and Carmine Croce supervised the oral history project: "This oral history project has been a learning experience for us, and a very rewarding one." Literacy/Basic Skills, The YMCA of Metropolitan Toronto, 15 Robina Avenue, Toronto, Ontario, M6C 3Y4.

Little by Little, Things Stick

This story was told by Hugo, a learner with the North Halton Literacy Guild, to Rila Hewer, his teacher. M. E. Evans was the co-ordinator and manager of the guild's oral history project: "I realized that the story the learner had to tell was in fact more interesting than if he had interviewed somebody else." North Halton Literacy Guild, P.O. Box 61, Georgetown, Ontario, L7G 4T1.

Who Am I?

This story was told by Vinci Giancola to Rosalind Cooke of the Impact-ASL Program of the Canadian Hearing Society. "The purpose of the Impact-ASL Program is to develop educational resources . . . to help students to be more aware of the deaf culture . . . and to preserve deaf history in Ontario [by collecting] the stories and folklore [of deaf people]." Impact-ASL Program, The Canadian Hearing Society, 271 Spadina Road, Toronto, M5R 2V3.

The Only Thing I Heard Was "Stupid"

This is a collection of excerpts from interviews conducted by students with fellow students at the Tri-County Literacy Council in Cornwall. Bruce Henbest was the co-ordinator of the group's oral history project: "The Tri-County Literacy Council undertook an oral history of the school experiences and memories of people who have had difficulty learning to read and write. School experiences and memories are virtually universal, but they are of particular interest to new readers who are necessarily trying to come to terms with their educational pasts." Tri-County Literacy Council, P.O. Box 522, Cornwall, Ontario, K6H 5T2.

Anybody's Dream

This story was told by Joe White to a participant in the Kingston Oral History Project, which was co-ordinated by Allison M. Harvey. Kingston Literacy, 88 Wright Crescent, Kingston, Ontario, K7L 4T9.

A Sobering Experience

This story was told by Vincent Murray to Sonya Smith and Freda Spice of the Prince Edward County Board of Education (Alternatives) Oral History Project. "The oral history group chose to do their project on Waupoos Island, an island off the southern shore of Prince Edward County. Many former residents of Waupoos Island have been interviewed, supplying us with a unique history of an island community in the late 1800s and early 1900s." Prince Edward County Alternatives, P.O. Box 1700, Picton, Ontario, K0K 2T0.

Thrown to the Floor and Stunned

This story was told by Hazel Pattermore Rowsome to Edna McRae of the Leeds/Grenville County Board of Education Oral History Project. Wendy Porteous is Supervisor of Adult Basic Education/ESL with the board: "[We have] approximately twenty hours of taped interviews — approximately 200 pages [of transcriptions]. . . . Anthology . . . selections [vary in] length and are written at a controlled level for both adult new readers and for students in the school system.

Numerous pictures and illustrations are included. . . . When the project is completed, a book containing both the anthology and transcriptions will be given to all literacy programs in our jurisdiction, as well as to the schools in our system. Copies of the tapes will also be available." Adult Basic Education/ESL, Leeds/Grenville County Board of Education, 25 Central Avenue West, Brockville, Ontario, K6V 5X1.

He Was a Dandy

This story was told by Lou Lavel to members of the St. Marys Adult Literacy Program. The oral history project was co-ordinated by Susannah Joyce. St. Marys Adult Literacy Program, Public Library, P.O. Box 700, St. Marys, Ontario, N0M 2V0.

All a Rat

This story was told by Donalda Kelly to participants in the oral history project of the Literacy Link of Eastern Ontario, which focused on the stories of women working in Kingston during the Second World War. "For literacy workers, the recording and interpretation of these fascinating stories was used to further develop and enhance students' literacy skills. For us [in the Kingston area], it's an important part of local and national history." Literacy Link of Eastern Ontario, 675 Bath Road, Lasalle Park Plaza, Kingston, Ontario, K7M 4X2.

A Woman Was Really a Slave

This story was told by Rachel Michaelis to Everett Walters of the Palmer Rapids Oral History Project, which was co-ordinated by Gwynne Foster. Renfrew County Outreach Literacy, c/o Gwynne Foster, R.R.2, Palmer Rapids, Ontario, K0J 2E0.

A Cruel Job

This story was told by Ron Judd to participants in the oral history project of the Haldimand-Norfolk Literacy Council. Susan Anderson was the co-ordinator of the project. Haldimand-Norfolk Literacy Council, 43 Kent Street North, Simcoe, Ontario, N3Y 3S1.

How to Play the Day

This story was told by Ivan Darling to L. Toop of the Leeds/Grenville County Board of Education Oral History Project. Wendy Porteus is Supervisor of Adult Basic Education/ESL with the board: "[We have] approximately twenty hours of taped interviews—approximately 200 pages [of transcriptions]. . . . Anthology . . . selections [vary in] length and are written at a controlled level for both adult new readers and for students in the school system. Numerous pictures and illustrations are included. . . . When the project is completed, a book containing both the anthology and transcriptions will be given to all literacy programs in our jurisdiction, as well as to the schools in our system. Copies of the tapes will also be available." Adult Basic Education/ESL, Leeds/Grenville County Board of Education, 25 Central Avenue West, Brockville, Ontario, K6V 5X1.

"M28"

This story was told by Edith Wood to participants in the oral history project of the Literacy Link of Eastern Ontario, which focused on the stories of women working in Kingston during the Second World War: "For literacy workers, the recording and interpretation of these fascinating stories was used to further develop and enhance students' literacy skills. For us [in the Kingston area], it's an important part of local and national history." Literacy Link of Eastern Ontario, 675 Bath Road, Lasalle Park Plaza, Kingston, Ontario, K7M 4X2.

As Unconcerned As Nothing

This story was told by C. M. Cosgrove to participants in the oral history project of the Literacy Link of Eastern Ontario, which focused on the stories of women working in Kingston during the Second World War: "For literacy workers, the recording and interpretation of these fascinating stories was used to further develop and enhance students' literacy skills. For us [in the Kingston area], it's an important part of local and national history." Literacy Link of Eastern Ontario, 675 Bath Road, Lasalle Park Plaza, Kingston, Ontario, K7M 4X2.

Just Gas

This story was told by Alva Turner to Diane Nicholls, a participant in the literacy program of the Community Resource Centre in Killaloe. The co-ordinators of the centre's oral history project were Kathlyn Lampi and Joanne Service. The project focused on pioneer women in Southwestern Renfrew County. "I love doing this, especially when it is easy to get the ladies to tell their stories." Community Resource Centre, P.O. Box 59, Killaloe, Ontario, K0J 2A0.

The Cat Got It

This story was told by Lena Marquard to Everett Walters of the Palmer Rapids Oral History Project, which was co-ordinated by Gwynne Foster. Renfrew County Outreach Literacy, c/o Gwynne Foster, R.R.2, Palmer Rapids, Ontario, K0J 2E0.

For Reasons of Taste and Pride

This story was told by Larry Pfaff to members of the St. Marys Adult Literacy Program. The oral history project was co-ordinated by Susannah Joyce. St. Marys Adult Literacy Program, Public Library, P.O. Box 700, St. Marys, Ontario, N0M 2V0.

Balm of Gilead

This story was told by Tom Sharbot to members of the Manomin Keezis Aboriginal Peoples Alliance. The group's oral history project was compiled and edited by Carol Pepper and Jennifer Tsun: "We represent Métis and off-reserve Native people in the Sharbot Lake area. We will be looking at many different aspects of how Native people in our area lived." The literacy program of the Manomin Keezis Aboriginal Peoples Alliance is no longer in operation.

Faster Than a Horse

This story was told by Adele Benedict to members of the Manomin Keezis Aboriginal Peoples Alliance. The group's oral history project was compiled and edited by Carol Pepper and Jennifer Tsun: "We represent Métis and off-reserve Native people in the Sharbot Lake area. We will be looking at many different aspects of how Native people in our area lived." The literacy program of the Manomin Keezis Aboriginal Peoples Alliance is no longer in operation.

Sometimes They Sing Another Song

This story was told by Jacob Loewen to participants in the oral history project of the Chatham-Kent Council on Basic Education. Margaret Rumble was the manager of the project. Chatham-Kent Council on Basic Education, 48 Fifth Street, Suite 303, Waymour Building, Chatham, Ontario, N7M 4V8.

The Great Days of Motoring

This story was told by John Barber to a participant in the oral history project of the North Halton Literacy Guild. The chosen topic for the project was "Georgetown Main Street". M. E. Evans was the co-ordinator and manager of the project: "[One interviewer] became very excited about interviewing, and also became very interested in local history and the paucity of material in the local archives. His horizons are widening and his confidence is increased, which surely demonstrates the value of this oral history project to facilitate learning." North Halton Literacy Guild, P.O. Box 61, Georgetown, Ontario, L7G 4T1.

"Kick the Can"

This story was told by Gerald Nolan to Heather Pelky, a member of the Niin Sakaan Literacy Program at the Indian Friendship Centre in Sault Ste. Marie. Florence Gray is Literacy Co-ordinator at the centre: "Gerald Nolan has spent all his life in Sault Ste. Marie and lives in the same house he was born in." Niin Sakaan Literacy Program, 114 Gore Street, Sault Ste. Marie, Ontario, P6A 1L9.

A Little Bit Better Than Before

This story was told by Manuel Da Silva to Carmine Croce of the YMCA Literacy Program of Toronto. Catherine O'Brien and Carmine Croce supervised the program's oral history project: "This oral history project has been a learning experience for us, and a very rewarding one." Literacy/Basic Skills, The YMCA of Metropolitan Toronto, 15 Robina Avenue, Toronto, Ontario, M6C 3Y4.

Is Anything Going to Happen Good to Me Today?

This story was told by Laurine Laughlin to Phillip Joudrey, a member of the Orillia and District Literacy Council. Edna Morris was the co-ordinator of the group's oral history project. Orillia and District Literacy Council, P.O. Box 41, Orillia, Ontario, L3V 6H9.

Acknowledgements

The Ministry of Education acknowledges the support of the National Literacy Secretariat of Multiculturalism and Citizenship Canada and the Archives of Ontario of the Ministry of Culture and Communications, which provided grants and resources for the Oral History Project, and wishes to thank Paul Yee of the Archives of Ontario for his support.

The Ministry of Education also wishes to acknowledge the contributions of the many organizations and individuals who participated in the Oral History Project of International Literacy Year, 1990, and in the development of this anthology. The contributors include the project co-ordinator, John Restakis, formerly with the Literacy Branch of the Ministry of Education and now with Alpha Consultants; the members of the twenty-eight community literacy programs that did oral history projects; Jenifer McVaugh, who selected and shaped the stories for inclusion in the anthology; the oral history trainers and consultants, including Cynthia Cohen from the Oral History Centre in Cambridge, Massachusetts, David Sobel, Joyce Wabano, Ranald Thurgood, Patrick O'Neill, and Brian Osborne; the

participants and trainers who attended the oral history retreat at Lake Couchiching; the Storylines editorial committee, comprising Mary Ellen Nurse, Joyce Wabano, Brian Osborne, and Susannah Joyce; all those who celebrated literacy at Harbourfront during the week of October 28 to November 3, 1990, by participating in events such as displays and presentations and in Story Visions, a reading evening on November 3; the Harbourfront Corporation, which co-sponsored Story Visions; and Ann Osborne, Mary Ellen Nurse, and Mary Breen of Storylinks: Learning Through Dialogue, the special interest group that will continue to promote the use of oral history as an integral part of community literacy practice.

Most of all the Ministry of Education wishes to acknowledge the contributions of the co-ordinators, tutors, and adult literacy learners who conducted the interviews in their communities, transcribed them, and collected relevant documentation, and the storytellers, the people in Ontario communities, often elders, who told their stories, many of which are included in this anthology.